Amazing Animals
Pandas

Please visit our web site at www.garethstevens.com.
For a free catalog describing our list of high-quality books, call 1-800-542-2595 (USA) or 1-800-387-3178 (Canada).
Our fax: 1-877-542-2596

Library of Congress Cataloging-in-Publication Data

Kueffner, Susan.
    Pandas / by Susan Kueffner.—U.S. ed.
          p. cm.—(Amazing Animals)
      Originally published: Pleasantville, NY: Reader's Digest Young Families, c2007.
      Includes bibliographical references and index.
      ISBN-10: 0-8368-9100-7   ISBN-13: 978-0-8368-9100-3 (lib. bdg.)
   1. Giant panda—Juvenile literature. I. Title.
QL737.C27K84 2009
599.789—dc22   2008013384

This edition first published in 2009 by
Gareth Stevens Publishing
A Weekly Reader® Company
1 Reader's Digest Road
Pleasantville, NY 10570-7000 USA

This edition copyright © 2009 by Gareth Stevens, Inc. Original edition copyright © 2006 by Reader's Digest Young Families, Pleasantville, NY 10570

Gareth Stevens Senior Managing Editor: Lisa M. Herrington
Gareth Stevens Creative Director: Lisa Donovan
Gareth Stevens Art Director: Ken Crossland
Gareth Stevens Associate Editor: Amanda Hudson

Consultant: Robert E. Budliger (Retired), NY State Department of Environmental Conservation

Photo Credits
Front cover: Digital Vision, Title page: iStockphoto.com/Michael Chen, Contents page: Tamir Niv/Shutterstock Inc., pages 6-7: Leonid Smirnov/ Shutterstock Inc., page 8: JupiterImages, page 9: Dynamic Graphics, Inc., page 10: Lynsey Allan/Shutterstock Inc., page 11: Digital Vision, page 12: Getty Images, pages 14-15: JupiterImages, page 16: iStockphoto.com/Sam Lee, page 19: iStockphoto.com/Dale Klonin, page 20: Ravshan Mirzaitov/Shutterstock Inc., page 21: Afarland/Shutterstock Inc., pages 22-23: Getty Images, page 24: iStockphoto.com/Andrei Tchernov, page 25: Wolong Panda Club & Pandas International, page 26: Christine Torres, page 27: Getty Images, page 28: iStockphoto.com/Terri Kieffer, pages 30-31: iStockphoto.com, page 33: Yu-Ju Lin/Shutterstock Inc., page 34: JupiterImages, page 36: iStockphoto.com/Paul Erickson, pages 38-39: JupiterImages, page 43: Leonid Smirnov/Shutterstock Inc., pages 44-45: iStockphoto.com/Markus Gregory, page 46: Dynamic Graphics, Inc., Back cover: iStockphoto.com/Dale Klonin.

Printed in the United States of America

1 2 3 4 5 6 7 8 9 10 09

Amazing Animals
Pandas

By Susan Kueffner

Gareth Stevens
Publishing
A WEEKLY READER COMPANY

Contents

Chapter 1
On the Bamboo Trail

Temporary Homes

A panda does not have a permanent **den**. It takes shelter in trees and caves as it looks for food.

"**G**rrrrr!" The sound of a snow leopard echoed through a forest in central China. The hungry leopard crouched on the ground. What was that up ahead? Was it just the snow? Or was something there?

From a tree limb high above, a giant panda watched and waited. An expert climber, the panda had scooted up the tree at the first sign of danger. She sat on the limb without making a sound. The leopard looked up. But the black patches of the panda's coat blended with the dark branches of the tree. The white patches disappeared into the light of the sky. Still hungry, the big cat walked on.

The snow began falling, but the panda wasn't cold. Her thick coat was warm and waterproof. After a time, she climbed down from the tree. She was hungry, too!

She walked slowly through the woods. Soon she came to a steep slope. She climbed up, using the hairy pads on her paws to grip the icy mountainside. From his perch high in a tree, a little red panda watched as she made the climb.

Family Ties

The red panda and the giant panda share the same **habitat**, the same diet, and the same name. Both animals are also **endangered**. But scientific tests place the red panda in the raccoon family and the giant panda in the bear family.

Sit Up Straight!

A panda sits up when it eats. This keeps its front paws free to hold the bamboo and pluck off the shoots and leaves.

When she got closer to the top of the mountain, she pushed through the trees and plants. Up ahead, a stream blocked her path. But wait! What was that? A patch of **bamboo** was growing on the other side. It was her favorite food! The panda waded into the water and swam across.

The panda broke stalks and leaves off a bamboo plant and sat down in the snow. Gripping the bamboo in her two front paws, she ate it all—stems, twigs, and leaves. She munched and crunched for hours.

When she was full, it was time to play. The panda slid down a hill on her back. She climbed back up the hill, pushed a rock down the slope, and chased after it.

After a while, the panda grew tired. She flopped to the ground and closed her eyes. Soon she would be hungry again, but now she would rest. It had been a very busy day.

Chapter 2
The Body of a Panda

Some scientists believe the giant panda is so special that it belongs in a family group all its own.

Is the Panda a Bear?

When European scientists first saw the giant panda in China, they were sure it was a kind of bear. But when the first skeleton of a panda was examined at a French museum, the scientists there disagreed. The skull and teeth were different, and it had a wrist bone that acted like a thumb. These scientists thought the panda belonged to the same family as the raccoon. This argument went on for more than 100 years, until tests performed in the 1980s showed that the giant panda has the same **DNA** as a bear.

A Spotty Story

According to a myth, the panda was once an all-white bear. A girl tried to save a panda cub from being attacked by a leopard. The leopard killed her instead. Pandas came to her funeral wearing armbands of black ashes in respect. As they wiped their eyes, hugged each other, and covered their ears, the pandas smudged the black ashes.

Of course, the panda's coloring is really nature's **camouflage**. The panda's coat blends into the dark rocks, white snow, and light skies of its mountain habitat.

Not So Cuddly

Pandas may look soft and cuddly, but their thick fur is stiff and oily. It protects against cold winters and keeps out water in the rainy climate of the Chinese forests.

A panda has a powerful body with a huge head, massive jaws, and short, thick legs. It has a short tail that is hidden away in the panda's fur.

Adult male pandas grow to be about 5 feet (1.5 meters) long from nose to tail and can weigh up to 220 pounds (100 kilograms). Females are a bit smaller—about 4 feet (1.2 m) long and 180 pounds (82 kg).

Pandas can stand upright, but they can't walk that way. Their short hind legs aren't strong enough to support their bodies. A panda's bones are twice as heavy as the bones of other animals the same size.

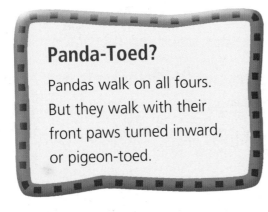

Panda-Toed?

Pandas walk on all fours. But they walk with their front paws turned inward, or pigeon-toed.

Giant pandas are walkers, not runners. With their weak hind legs, a slow trot is as fast as they can go!

Pandas are expert tree climbers. They can sit in the branches for hours.

Green Is Good!

Pandas prefer to eat the softer shoots and leaves of bamboo. But they'll eat the woody stalks if they have to.

Thumbs Up

A panda's front paws have special features that help it eat bamboo, its favorite food. The five clawed "fingers" on each paw are lined up in a row, which makes it easy to whack through the bamboo stalks. The front paws also have large wrist bones that act as thumbs. They help the panda grab and hold on.

Chew on This!

Bamboo is a tall and woody kind of grass. It is often so tough that humans need an ax to cut through it. Imagine trying to bite, chew, and swallow it! But it's no problem for pandas, thanks to sharp teeth used for biting and large flat teeth (molars) used for crushing their food. Pandas also have huge jaw muscles that are strong enough to chew through metal.

Tough to Swallow

A panda has special linings in its throat and stomach that allow it to swallow splintery bamboo stalks without being hurt.

Chapter 3
Mothers and Cubs

Pandas are shy. They choose to live most of their lives alone, except in the spring when they look for mates.

Looking for a Mate

Scent plays an important part in bringing pandas together to start a family. A six-year-old female panda is fully grown and ready to have a baby. She announces this to male pandas by spraying urine and rubbing the scent **glands** located under her tail against tree trunks and rocks. Male pandas leave scent marks the same way. They sniff and follow these scent trails until they find one another.

Bear Hugs

A female panda is choosy about her mate. She might turn her back and run from a male that doesn't appeal to her. She might cuff him with her paw or bite him! The male may try to change her mind by climbing a tree and calling out a song of low barks. Sometimes several males will find one female at the same time. The female usually chooses the biggest and strongest one.

Most pandas mate sometime between March and May. Then they go their separate ways. About five months later, the female will find a den in a hollow tree or cave and give birth to one or two tiny babies.

A Hard Choice

If twin babies are born, only one will survive. A mother panda is not able to care for two cubs at one time, and so she must choose the stronger one.

Tender, Loving Care

A mother panda holds her tiny baby close to her body to keep him warm. She never puts her baby down. She feeds him milk almost every hour. Mother and cub stay in the den for two or more weeks. Scientists do not understand exactly how a mother panda can go so long without food.

When the mother is so hungry that she has to leave the den, she carries the cub in one of her front paws or in her mouth. She cradles the baby in her paw while she eats bamboo to keep up her strength.

By the end of the first month, the baby panda has all his spots. His eyes begin to open when he is four to six weeks old. They don't fully open until he is seven weeks old. He is still very tiny!

In the Pink

A newborn panda is the size of a newborn kitten. It has pink skin, a thin coat of white fur, a long tail, and no teeth. Its eyes are closed.

Big Mama!

A mother panda is about 900 times bigger than her newborn baby!

Mother and child spend lots of time together. They cuddle, play, and eat bamboo. They are constant companions until the cub is about two.

Growing Up ...
and Out!

A baby panda is almost two months old before he is the size of an average human newborn baby. He spends most of his day doing what human babies do—drinking milk. But a panda can crawl, stand, and take his first steps at three months of age. That's long before a human baby can do those things. His first teeth appear then, too.

At three or four months, the cub is playful. He can roll around and climb on his mother's back. At five months, he can walk, trot, and climb trees. His adult teeth come in at six months. He starts eating more solid foods, but he does not stop drinking his mother's milk until he is nine months old.

The following year is spent with his mother—roaming, playing, and eating. The baby continues to grow until he weighs about 220 pounds (100 kg) at age two. Now fully grown, the young panda leaves his mother for a life of his own. Between the ages of four and eight, he will be ready to mate. Then the panda's cycle of life starts again.

Chapter 4
The Life of a Wanderer

One-Dish Dinners

You may be surprised to learn that pandas are **carnivores** (meat eaters) by nature, but **vegetarians** by habit. They'll eat meat if they come upon the leftovers of another meat-eating animal's meal. Every now and then they will grab fish from a stream. But pandas move too slowly to hunt. Their favorite food is bamboo. And they like lots of it!

Pandas do eat other kinds of plants, like mushrooms and flowers. They also love honey. But there are hundreds of different kinds of bamboo, and they're easy to find, even when it snows. And there aren't many other bamboo-eaters to compete with.

Bamboo is low in **nutrients**. The giant panda has to eat many pounds of bamboo every day just to stay alive.

The panda spends 14 to 16 hours every day eating bamboo.

Wild Words

Bears that **hibernate** go into a deep, sleeplike state over the winter months. They live off body fat that they have stored up. Pandas cannot store enough body fat to hibernate.

The panda's Chinese habitat, lush with bamboo all year round, is called the "bamboo belt."

In the Woods

Pandas roam the rainy mountain forests of central China. Grown pandas establish their own territories. This is where they live and look for food. Males wander over larger distances, overlapping the territories of several females. Some scientists believe they prefer to roam at twilight or in the dark, sleeping just before dawn and in the afternoon.

At one time scientists called giant pandas "hermits of the forest." They thought the bears tried to avoid one another. But recent studies show that pandas overlap one another's home territories. They are aware of their neighbors by the scent markings the neighbors have left behind.

Unlike bears that hibernate in the winter, pandas are on the move all year long. That's because their food is available year-round and is not very nutritious. Pandas can't eat enough bamboo to fatten up for a long winter's rest. When the weather turns really cold, pandas travel to the valleys, where it's warmer. They will return to the chillier mountainsides in summer, when the heat becomes too much for their fur coats.

Pandas will lie down almost anywhere during the day to take a nap.

The Strong, Silent Type

Pandas do not need to make many different sounds because they spend most of their time alone. In fact, the quieter they are, the less likely they are to attract attention and the more likely they are to find the peace and quiet they like.

When they do have something to say, pandas can communicate. They don't roar like bears, though. They bleat like sheep! This is a kind of greeting. They might bark like a dog to attract a mate or make a honking sound when scared. Young pandas squeal like human babies when they want attention.

Pandas can raise a noisy fuss when they find other pandas in their territory. Then they might huff or growl to warn them to stay away.

Calls of the Wild Panda

Panda researchers have counted 11 different panda calls—and four of them are used only when searching for a mate.

Chapter 5

Pandas in the World

Where Pandas Live

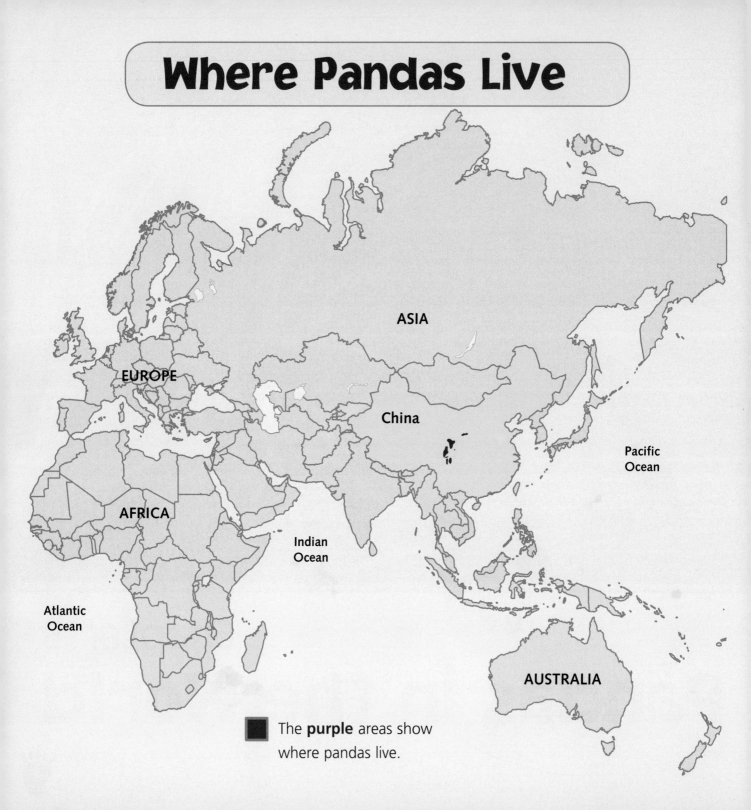

ASIA

EUROPE

China

Pacific
Ocean

AFRICA

Indian
Ocean

Atlantic
Ocean

AUSTRALIA

The **purple** areas show
where pandas live.

People and Pandas

Pandas have lived in the world for two to three million years. In ancient China, pandas were thought to have magical powers. These rare animals were kept by Chinese emperors, and their prized **pelts** were given as gifts.

The rest of the world discovered the panda only in 1869. That was when a French scientist sent a pelt and skeleton back to a natural history museum in Paris. It created a sensation. Demand for the beautiful animal sent hundreds of hunters and animal dealers to China. People wanted skins for museums and live pandas for zoos. Hunting and the cutting down of forests to create farms have made the panda one of the most endangered animals in the world.

Today, there are only about 20 small groups of pandas living in the mountain ranges of three provinces in China: Sichuan, Gansu, and Shaanxi. Studies estimate that there are as few as 1,000 pandas left in the world.

The Future of Pandas

The Chinese government considers the panda a national treasure and is trying to protect it. Hunting pandas was outlawed in the 1960s. Logging in the panda's habitat has been banned. The government has also set up **preserves** for the panda.

Still, China is home to more than a billion people. There are 85 million people in Sichuan alone, trying to feed themselves by farming. The World Wildlife Fund and other groups are working with the government to help farmers develop ecofriendly businesses, such as **ecotourism**.

Fast Facts About Pandas

Scientific name	*Ailuropoda melanoleuca*
Class	Mammalia
Order	Carnivora
Weight	Males up to 220 pounds (100 kg) Females up to 180 pounds (82 kg)
Life span	14 to 20 years in the wild; up to 30 in captivity
Habitat	Mountain forests in central China

Pandas have become the symbol
of the World Wildlife Fund and of
endangered animals everywhere.

Glossary

bamboo — a plant with long, woody, often hollow stems and tender shoots and leaves

camouflage — colors and patterns on an animal that help it blend in with its surroundings

carnivore — a meat-eating animal

den — place where a wild animal sleeps or rests

DNA — coded material in the cells of living things that determines what they look like and how they act and is passed down to their offspring

ecotourism — travel tours that encourage preservation of areas visited

endangered — in danger of extinction

gland — a part of the body that makes chemicals and often releases them, sometimes as a scent

habitat — the natural environment where an animal or plant lives

nutrients — the parts of food that help an animal stay healthy and grow

pelt — the fur and skin of an animal

preserve — an area of land where wildlife and plants are protected

vegetarian — eats only food from plants

Pandas:
Show What You Know

How much have you learned about pandas? Grab a piece of paper and a pencil and write your answers down.

1. What is a panda's favorite food?

2. How many hours a day does a panda spend eating?

3. Why don't pandas hibernate like other bears?

4. In what country are pandas found in the wild?

5. How long can mother pandas go without food after their babies are born?

6. Why can't pandas walk on their hind legs?

7. How old are pandas when they leave their mothers?

8. Why did scientists once call pandas "hermits of the forest"?

9. What two major factors have led to pandas' becoming endangered?

10. About how many pandas are left in the world today?

1. Bamboo 2. 14-16 3. They can't store enough body fat. 4. China 5. Two or more weeks 6. Their hind legs aren't strong enough to support them. 7. 2 years old 8. Because they thought pandas tried to avoid one another. 9. Hunting and the cutting down of forests 10. 1,000

For More Information

Books

Giant Pandas. Wild Ones (series). Anderson, Jill (NorthWord Books, 2006)

Giant Pandas. Amazing Animals (series). Cruickshank, Don (Weigl Publishers, 2006)

Giant Pandas. Pull Ahead Books–Animals (series). Levine, Michelle (Lerner Publishing Group, 2006)

Web Sites

Mammals: Giant Panda

http://www.sandiegozoo.org/animalbytes/t-giant_panda.html

This site provides all kinds of fun and interesting panda facts, along with a blog by the San Diego Zoo's Giant Panda Team and video of pandas in action.

Pandas

http://www.worldwildlife.org/pandas

Would you like to adopt a panda? The World Wildlife Fund offers opportunities to help pandas survive and thrive. Visit its site for information on this and other endangered species.

Publisher's note to educators and parents: Our editors have carefully reviewed these Web sites to ensure that they are suitable for children. Many Web sites change frequently, however, and we cannot guarantee that a site's future contents will continue to meet our high standards of quality and educational value. Be advised that children should be closely supervised whenever they access the Internet.

Index